Stolen Halo's

Flame

authorHOUSE®

AuthorHouse™
1663 Liberty Drive
Bloomington, IN 47403
www.authorhouse.com
Phone: 1 (800) 839-8640

Published by AuthorHouse 03/31/2016

ISBN: 978-1-5049-8670-0 (sc)
ISBN: 978-1-5049-8669-4 (e)

Library of Congress Control Number: 2016904807

Print information available on the last page.

Any people depicted in stock imagery provided by Thinkstock are models, and such images are being used for illustrative purposes only. Certain stock imagery © Thinkstock.

This book is printed on acid-free paper.

Dedication

I would like to say, that if it wasn't for my mother Ruth
Lott, I couldn't put two words together.
and my brother George Finan, for the graphics of this book.
And my Aunt Ginger and Uncle Bill Ritchie, for believing that
I can do this book as well as handling everyday life.
And last but not least, my Wife Linda who has stood by me for the last four years.
God has blessed me with all of you, and I pray for you to
receive the same.

For all of you this book is for you!
Flame!

My uncle Bill is responsible for this book.
I cannot say it any other way.
The man has given me countless computers that he built himself.
He also gave me the wisdom of its okay.
Meaning
If it turns out the way you want it's okay.
In life does not turn out the way you want it's okay.
In his actions he actually showed me it's okay!
It really makes me feel bad when he says, I'm ready for the pine box.
Although I have to say, I really know what he means.
He has done his chores here on earth.
And he has proven his worth.
So anybody that thinks I deserve this book?
Please give my uncle Bill a 2nd look!
Uncle Bill thank you and God bless you for helping me make out
who I am!

Flame! ☺

Table of Contents

I Have a Purpose

I have a purpose it's to start the fire someone's heart.
To put sparkle back someone's eye.
It's to catch someone before they fall.
To make friends with someone that doesn't like me.
My purpose is to be the hand that dries the tear
of an old lady.
It's to find the child that's lost.
It's to be godlike even though I will never be God.
When everyone is looking at the rocks I am looking
at the pebbles underneath them.
It's to give some faith to those without.
It's to give people something to look up to at eye level.
It's to give a smile without a tear.
It to sacrifice everything for nothing.
It's to be someone's light when all is door.
Just to hold someone's hand whenever they are scared.
My purpose is to simply understand.
My purpose is to love endlessly no matter what!

By
Flame

Flame! ✿❦☺

The Dream Remains

When I was a child I had a dream of being the best.
But as I got older somehow I put that to rest.
It's still here way in the back of my mind.
Trying to recall that dream is very hard I find.
In my mind is hard to find the pieces to put back together.
But honestly I don't think it's gone forever.
In my life I've been soiled with many stains.
But I have no doubts that the dream remains!
I will be glad to let you know what it is I recall.
I feel it's a greatness that never will fall.
Truth prevails and the foolishness is no more.
It's just hard for me to believe that you can lose
because it's within you deep in your core.
Passion love and your soul, together with your mind.
I try to focus on all of these and leaving none of them behind.
And if you walk tall be nice yet need to use a cane
just try hard to remember, your dream remains!
When I said I want to be the best I meant in every realm
of the way.
Ecstasy awaits us I tell you the truth.
And yes that's the one thing I have not forgot about my youth.
I don't want to be a hero with metals on my chest.
For myself at 52 I just want to know that I am the best.
Say what you want be what you want but be willing to work for it hard.
My point is that even if you get dealt a bad hand in
this life to you.
Not to talk you into anything, but down my cheek
rolls a joyful tear that I cannot refrain.
And after all I have been through I know,
the dream remains!!!

By
Flame

Flame!☺

- 2 -

I Failed

God forgive me I walked down the wrong trail.
Forgive me oh Lord for I have failed.
As many times as I tried to do good to others.
So often I tried to spread the love amongst my brothers.
I have one tear left that needs to be caught.
There is one more miracle than needs to be sought.
Just give me the chance and I will do what I have to do.
For anybody that knows me knows you.
Given this chance I think I can do it right.
Because truly in me I feel the light.
Surely you are not the one I want to go against.
Honest God, I think you are so intense.
Lord please do not let me become un railed
for God's sakes do not tell me I failed.
Please just pick me up and let me be held.
I fear the words though I fail.
All my life I have given my best.
Here I stand your worst child.
And yet for you I don't get pretty wild.
Your protection I truly need.
And this I truly think you can conceive.
Just give me that chance the one you said you would.
Let the world know that I am here for you.
For my powerfulness through you this is what I can do.
Oh sweetness take off the veil.
And let the world know I failed!

By
Flame

Flame!🌹☺

Never will

I can't get my brain to work with my emotions or how I feel.
I don't understand now and probably never will.
There is a love bursting inside of me to share it with all.
Some tell me that may be my call.
A wise man told me one time that is not what I think it's what I do.
And to some extent I have to say that's true.
Through drugs and alcohol I made my mind so still.
I might get it back but maybe I never will.
I cry out loud for the words come so fast.
And that means there were times that I just crashed.
There are things in this world that I think of that are irrelevant to
all the others!
I can't balance out fantasy and reality between me and another.
I am preoccupied with myself as you can see.
But regardless of the words I speak it's not all about me.
I have faith in God and now know where I am supposed to
be right now.
I just don't understand, but before him I bow!
Maybe it is about me, because me myself and I want to please
God so badly!
I am a human being, so this I probably could not perform, so sadly.
Here's the only thing that I think I'm trying to sell.
For me to turn away from God, I never will!

By
Flame

Flame!

Know This

I am not big, but my concept is great, powerful and extremely hard to understand.
Retract my brain and you might have a clue.
Because between the two of them it all comes down
to loving you.
There is a great silence between me and my words.
I thank mostly it's my heart because of how many times
it's been hurled.
Frolicking in a world I don't belong.
So I make my own music and even sing along.
Being knocked the down I always seem to get up again.
And some of the people I know are the worst, and yet they are still my friend.
Well in my opinion there is no reason to clench your fist.
If you can't understand anything in this page then you have nothing left but rage.
Know this!
Your emotions cannot go any further than you let them just
so you know.
You are a fool to say I can stand toe to toe.
Stop your brain and see the contrast between that
and your heart.
It's just like getting your car fixed and forgetting
an important part.
We may cry tears of some things that are hard to understand.
They both complement each other and that is so grand.
If you forget about God or to speaking with him?
You will notice your light is getting dim,
if you feel your life has no more of that bless?
Got is the answer and you should,
know this!

By
Flame

Flame!🌿☺

For You I Can

I've been in the dumps and always seemed
I could prevail.
And when I met you, I thought to myself my ship is
about to sale.
The first time I saw you I felt as if I was going to melt.
And until the day you walked out the door this is
how I felt.
You say I am a drunk and that I am no man.
Through heart felt tears I say to you, for you I can.
Right down to this painful day I do believe in you.
And honestly I always well, even though people tell
me not to.
Like it or not I gave you my life and so much more.
You brock my heart broke me down and then,
walked out the door.
I try to tell people how beautiful you really are and how in you I can confide.
But my only reply from them is how I lied.
How will you take it the day you asked about me and they say I have died.
Would you say I can't help that? Would that
be your plan?
Because if you wanted me back in your life I think somehow for you I can!

By
Flame

Flame! ☺

Endure this

The first time my eyes laid up on you.
Immediately my heart said to me this is true.
You asked for it, so I gave you a kiss.
It was so intense I had to say to myself, how
do I Endure this?
Seeing you there in front of me I just
wanted a touch.
Truly I loved you that much.
At that moment I had no concept as
to what was fair.
And to this day I'll take on anything you dare.
I have been shot, stabbed, and hung and as well.
But when I met you is when I fell.
You left me here to understand all this.
So my sweet lady how do I Endure this?
I sweat bullets every time you walk into the room.
You make it hard for me to understand I
once was your groom.
You say I drink too much and I know that is right.
So now mother is angry and friends are
out of sight.
I beg of you don't just leave me here alone.
Please baby, be my rock just, see me when
I am not stoned.
I cry to you as I am clinching my fist.
I beg of you, just tell me baby how
do I Endure this?

By
Flame

Flame! ❀☺

Fall out!

I've had a thought all my life every day.
If you'd like to know about it, let me tell you it
went this way.
A horrible thing came into my soul.
It got there when I was in my youth and it's still there now that I'm old.
Someone told me that's the way I look at it.
and that thought still hurts quite a bit.
It's been a life time, thinking on how this came about.
I wake up at times and then I just fall out!
There is a great thunder within my heart, and lightning streaks through my brain.
Some say I'm great, and others think I'm insane.
Love is a word I've never known.
But I can say at least I've grown.
Maybe what it is that took me a long time ago?
People can't understand or even want to know.
I try to be godlike at least.
and all too often I feel that beast.
I've always been told I will reap the garden that I sow.
Not too often in my lifetime I get to see myself grow.
My life is getting dark and soon the lights will
be turned out.
I just want to face it all, just don't want to be the one who will fall out!
I cannot serve two masters this I know.
My chances of survival are slim but I think I know which way to go.
It is hell what people do to me.
But it's not their fault how would they now
what it's about.
Maybe I should stop emotions and those great thoughts, and just fall out!!!

By
Flame

Flame!

Shot Down

I count on you so many times.
Somehow I feel like it's a crime.
To please you I always did.
You had me right from the beginning as a kid.
let's stop this foolishness and get to the point.
But I feel when you point the finger it is my point.
And not I understand on my home ground.
Jesus Christ I never thought I would be shot down.
I've never lost my faith not at all.
Although sometimes I need some help to figure
out my call.
You put pressure on me I just can't stand.
I feel like he tried to make me more than a man.
Shot down in the dark I guess that's the way it's supposed to be.
Let me tell you right now I can take it like it should.
But if somebody gave me I have a chance I might be what I could.
I don't cry because clouds are in the sky.
There are clouds in the sky because I cry.
Let's quit all this bull and get right down to it.
My brain just doesn't get it.
Some say am smart some say I'm dumb.
I just assume my day is going to come.
I am so confused with the truth.
And it has always been so since my youth.
But this is what I have found.
I truly have been shot down.
No guns involved none at all.
Just the insanity is called.
So I let it go every bit.
And upon my life you can spit.
And my life is certainly can frown.
Because honestly it has been shot down.
I thought all the King but he showed me different.
I really wasn't anything insignificant.
God I wish I could show you what I know now.
For you would drop everything that you're doing and bow down.
Because you would find out how, I was shot down!

By
Flame

The Power in Us

Verse one
We are just two old guys something to discuss.
Verse two
We just want to pass on the power in us.
Verse three
Just want to give you something in which you can pass on!
Verse four
When we leave here we are not necessarily gone.
Chorus
It's not me or him, and don't make it into a fuss.
You got that same power that is in us!
All we want to do is make this a plus!
Understand, we want you to have the power in us!
Repeat the whole song.

By
Flame

Flame!🌹☺

Let' Just Stop

We have many rules and regulations in this institution.
I think we are all lost and have no solution.
There are no leaders they are all just on top.
I say leave it be, and lets just stop!
Children are raised by fear.
Not forgetting all the tears.
We destroy the farmers and their crop.
So here's my concept let's just stop.
As far as from the east to the west.
We are arrogant enough to say we are the best.
The answer gets close you know, with a skip,
jump, and a hop.
So I say once more, please, let's just stop.
Our heroes are now on their knees.
But we are not weak, if we can just see.
That our lives, comes from the heart.
If we can do that it truly is a start.
There is a way for us to be on top.
The answer to this can only be, let's just stop.
We merely need to cry at times.
Give of yourself, not just your nickels and dimes.
Make up for all the times you forgot.
And know this, let's just stop.

By
Flame

Flame!☺

Lost!

I was born within a bitter frost.
But you know, I seemed to have quickly gotten lost.
My early childhood, I found myself in such great pain.
And last night I had that nightmare again.
It seems that it just won't ever go away.
I have no choice, it comes back every day.
My mind, my heart, and every bit of my soul.
The bustard took me down, he took all
of me so cold.
I am told to not think about it, it's all in the past.
Remember all those good things that were a blast.
So I say, but I did pay for everything and at such a cost.
And now my whole life is lost.
She brought me back to the man I use to be.
And so I feel once again that chilling frost
coming onto me.
Will she love me right till the end.
Or is she a far wither friend.
That love that she offers is nothing but for her.
And yet, there is something I try to deter.
There is nothing, and absolutely at any cost.
I wouldn't pay to not be lost.
But, she is gone as she gives my heart toss.
And here I sit totally lost!

By
Flame

Flame!

Tangled love

In no manner did I think it would be this way.
And yet, the woman I fell in love with is not
with me today.
Not that she passed away or anything like that.
But to her I am nothing more than
an aggravating nat.
I'm not sure if I was not enough or way too much.
However, I don't think she could deny that I gave
her that loving touch.
I have tried to teach her about all the sin.
But these days I only see darkness within.
I tried to be understanding and not too tough.
The whole time, I was trying to fix
our tangled love.
The craziness of it all, is we can't say goodbye
to one another.
And I truly want a wife, but she just wants a lover.
A broken heart, and emotions that will not quit, it's really getting awfully rough.
I just don't know if I can repair this tangled love.
It's almost like a drug that won't wear off.
But she is awesomely soft.
Her heart was broken way in the past.
And I guess to her I couldn't mend it well enough to last.
She is really soft spoken but, honestly
I speak, very gruff.
Let me tell you this is one tangled love.
So when she makes her peace and goes to church.
Her heart, I pray she asks God to search.
Sincerely, I can talk forever about all of this stuff.
But, I can no longer save this tangled love.

By
Flame

Flame!☺

A silent tear

Since I was a young boy, a broken heart was
my greatest fear.
And so I cried a silent tear.
And so I grew in the world I knew.
Yes, I understood that this would come true.
It's relevant how I thought it would come
about some day.
But I could see all the pain coming my way.
All my life I knew I should not flirt.
For I knew nothing knew my heart would
Feel that hurt.
So if you listen you just might hear.
Something I call a silent tear.
She came into my life with the beauty and elegance.
It all was so extremely intense.
To my heart, and it blew my mind away.
I can tell you the words I remember every day.
I asked, will you marry me and her reply was, yes dear.
And so began the crying of a silent tear!

By
Flame

Flame!🌿☺

Be Still

When problems attack you and this is how you feel.
The only two words that can correct that is be still.
I've been shot by the arrow of love and it took its toll.
Take it like a man and try your best and be still.
Don't let revenge run through your veins.
Take it from a man, for that will only leave your heart with pain.
Today I have too much distraught on this day and cannot explain
the way I feel.
But there is a truth to all this I'm sure to explain it, and I will.
With the mass confusion all around us.
There are so many things that we should discuss.
There is an experience of in my life and it's for real.
Let me start at the beginning it's imperative that we be still.
Focus; if it is done correctly you will see the appeal.
Anger is not needed to get in the way I am sure.
Hope you had a great day and with a smile he replies says yes that's what I say.
A smile and a handshake a comment that is so nice.
I now I have enemies, but to make a friend I will sacrifice.
Launch the bomb of pleasure and I think you will find the treasure.
Extraordinarily, the heart always seems to win.
So now I will tell you the big secret of having it nice.
It is never what you receive only that which you sacrifice.
So please allow me to let you know what is true and real.
Be still

By
Flame

Flame!🌹☺

Set myself free

Here I sit looking at the stars.
Looking for that place that is not ours.
Looking for that place for my soul.
Finding that place called Paradise this is my goal.
My own thoughts bewilder me as you can tell.
Psychotic thinking is the reason I fell.
Did I somehow just fall on the earth?
And can somebody tell me what I am worth?
My emotions take over My Space.
The only thing I've ever learned in my life, is I don't belong
in this place!
I cry out for your help and try to get you to see.
All I ever wanted was to set myself free.

By
Flame

Flame!☺

I Will Always Catch Your Tears

I never meant to hurt you or cause you dismay.
My dreams for you never wanted it to
turn out this way.
Pain for you, is something that I try to refrain!
You have nothing to lose and everything to gain.
I will never again allow you to have any more fears.
And my sweetness, I will always catch
your tears!
My heart is always here for you to have.
And since I met you, all I want to do is make you laugh.
God has blessed me with the beauty you aspire.
Every time you come into my view, all I can think is
it's you I desire.
You are all that my soul ever hears.
So honey, understand this, I will always catch your tears!

By
Flame

Flame! ☺

Such a Cost

Born a winter baby I was fresh as snow.
And growing up I seem to grasp so slow.
Although in my life things seem
to come easy.
And yet people seem to be blind because no one
could see me.
Some would call me a genius,
yet it was unknown.
My emotions took control of me and
this was known.
Now my heart is covered in frost.
I lost that life at such a cost!

By
Flame

Flame!🌹☺

The Dream Remains

When I was a child I had a dream of being the best.
But as I got older somehow I put that to rest.
It's still here way in the back of my mind.
Trying to recall that dream is very hard I find.
In my mind is hard to find the pieces to put back together.
But honestly I don't think it's gone forever.
In my life I've been soiled with many stains.
But I have no doubts that the dream remains!
I will be glad to let you know what it is I recall.
I feel it's a greatness that never will fall.
Truth prevails and the foolishness is no more.
It's just hard for me to believe that you can lose
because it's within you deep in your core.
Passion love and your soul, together with your mind.
I try to focus on all of these and leaving none of them behind.
And if you walk tall be nice yet need to use a cane
just try hard to remember, your dream remains!
When I said I want to be the best I meant in every realm
of the way.
Ecstasy awaits us I tell you the truth.
And yes that's the one thing I have not forgot about my youth.
I don't want to be a hero with metals on my chest.
For myself at 52 I just want to know that I am the best.
Say what you want be what you want but be willing to work for it hard.
My point is that even if you get dealt a bad hand in
this life to you.
Not to talk you into anything, but down my cheek
rolls a joyful tear that I cannot refrain.
And after all I have been through I know,
the dream remains!!!

By
Flame

Flame!🌹☺

A Gift

I always thought I had to sweat it out.
With the empathy I felt for the others there is no doubt.
and I am not dumb but not swift.
I really don't get this but they say I have a gift.
What is so simple for others, to me it gets really complicated.
As I watch my life, become so close to being faded.
But I see God stretching down to give me a left.
For God truly gave me a gift!
And now I truly understand how it is supposed to be.
To let you know that you are free.
In some way it's up to me to give you a lift.
And Not to brag, but this is a gift!
Desperate I am, to fix all of this.
I just might be that Angel who swoops down to give
you Gods kiss!
I am here for you, I am here for you so don't think I am not a drift.
So slow down and allow me to pass on this, a gift!

By
Flame

Flame!

Cried

We all are children but no two alike.
There are also special and precious in our site.
Someone told me one time don't tell a soul.
But sometimes they play another role.
Here it comes again? Those same old emotions that blows
our mind right?
But that's when I start to see my light.
Everything I know in my head became a lie.
So, I cried!
And thank God every time I fell I got up again.
I was about to love all my family and friends.
And I am learning that there is always someone you can confide.
I saw the spirit and I cried.
It's not like everything is just great.
For some of us that's just not our fate!
And this comes from a mind that is fried.
And because of that, I cried!

By
Flame

Flame! 🌹☺

For You I Can

I've been in the dumps and always seemed
I could prevail.
And when I met you, I thought to myself my ship is
about to sale.
The first time I saw you I felt as if I was going to melt.
And until the day you walked out the door this is
how I felt.
You say I am a drunk and that I am no man.
Through heart felt tears I say to you, for you I can.
Right down to this painful day I do believe in you.
And honestly I always well, even though people tell
me not to.
Like it or not I gave you my life and so much more.
You brock my heart broke me down and then,
walked out the door.
I try to tell people how beautiful you really are and how in you I can confide.
But my only reply from them is how I lied.
How will you take it the day you asked about me and they say I have died.
Would you say I can't help that? Would that
be your plan?
Because if you wanted me back in your life I think somehow for you I can!

By
Flame

Flame!☙☺

- 22 -

Broke

I've been broken in my life many times it seems.
But I never was broke of my dreams.
Today is deferent I must say.
The child is grown and the dreams all have gone.
Now all that's left to do is pray from dusk to dawn.
Lost in this place and new to another.
And all I can take are the words of my brother.
If I can't find my way, it's my own dam fault.
Because with in the bible, I never read a lot.
It would have told me just how I feel inside.
And how we are here for the ride.
Yes I have felt left out, and was the butt of many a joke.
But I am a man that has never been
Broke!

By
Flame

Yet

Fifty and all I have left is deduction.
A tear in my eye, from my own reflection.
I was told of a fire red sunset.
God only knows I have not seen one yet.
Tell you what, a colorful butterfly landing on the
bud of a yellow rose.
I have never, came across one of those.
I wanted to run free and shoot for the sky.
But somehow that just passed me by.
I cried in the night, to tell my brother all my regrets.
But I have not told him as of yet.
To lay across the breast of a God that
only I could understand.
And someone told me Mr., please don't fret.
This day will come for you yet.
I have not heard the flutter of an unborn
child's heartbeat.
I do live with the right and wrong that I do!
So, here is the question that I present to you.
When I step off of this cloud, to clear up all my debt.
With love rushing through my veins, and rivers for
tears flowing down, you can truly bet!!!
I will say dear sweet God, can I come home yet!

By
Flame

Flame!❀⚡☺

Betrayal of a Friend

Tears fell and I was not there to catch them.
When it was dark I did not shine my light.
When you needed help I had forsaken you.
When you wanted truth I gave you lies.
When you needed someone to catch you, I could not look you in the eyes.
It's sad to think of life's end.
All I became is the betrayal of a friend.
When your heart was braking I could not mend it.
When you needed honesty I only bent it.
When your soul was in need?
I did no good deeds.
The laughter you tried to share.
I couldn't seem to bare.
It's so sad that in the end.
All I was? Was the betrayal of a friend.
Life seems to twist and turn.
And all I've done is make it burn.
All of this is nothing but fake.
And I've given you all you can take.
Yes it is all so sad at life's end.
For all I am, is the betrayal of a friend!!!
You gave me everything a man could want.
And your memories for me will always taunt.
The truth will go with me when I descend.
And a single tear for the betrayal of a friend.

By
Flame

You Spoke I Heard

You made me cry right down to my last tear drop.
But when I saw you I thought my heart would pop!
Every day with you makes me feel like, my head
is all blurred.
Outrageously though, you spoke I heard!
You took away my pain and deep distress too.
And I should do so much more for you!
It seems to me, what has occurred.
And no matter what if you spoke I heard!
That sparkling eye of yours gets me every time you see?
I like to see you laugh and act so free.
So the pure simple things we have endured.
But the important thing is, if you spoke I heard!

By
Flame

Flame!☺

Heartless Man

He came across a woman that he loved so dear.
Whenever she was around he had in him no fear.
The strength within him came from inside.
So one day he asked her to be his bride.
But soon she would no longer play that part.
He felt very foolish and not very smart.
So walking through life, without feelings
like most people can.
Truly she turned him into a heartless man!
Emptiness is the promise he holds for tomorrow.
His face is soft and yet full of sorrow.
Trapped in a cage his emotions are not to show.
Because this, he will not grow.
For her, there is not anything he would not try!
He would give her anything she wanted, even
the colors of the sky.
Nothing left inside of him as she walks on.
She made sure she had it all before she was gone.
Just look into his eyes if you dare or even can.
For all you will see these days is a heartless man.
All of his hopes where taken on that day.
All his dreams where crushed that very same way.
There is no doubt that he's been dead for some time.
He still walks around trying to make sense of this crime.
A whole now, is where there used to be a very big heart that ran.
A tear rolls down my cheek for this heartless man.

By
Flame

Flame!❦☺

Chased you Till You Caught Me

I've never seen anything so beautiful in my life.
That even comes close to my wife.
Given this day I will never say.
She has tripped me up this way.
Altogether, she has made me feel so free.
I chased you till you caught me.
It's really easy to tell.
That I have truly been through my hell.
I have given you my ultimate truth.
I've told you all about me, even my youth.
I have sent my wisdom to you.
I give you my freedom sure as hell.
I'm hoping you will understand this as well.
I would never forget you not on this day.
Forgive me for thing in this way.
Would you love me this way.
Shamed or not, this is how I feel.
Can you give me something that is real.
Your cascade eyes should be mine,
I cannot see another.
I should be able to but I cannot see another.
Honey, all I got to say is as far as me.
I chased you till you caught me!

By
Flame

Flame!🌹☺

I don't Want You To End

You took me in when no one else could seem to handle it.
You truly loved me, every little bit.
You gave me confidence when I really had none.
Mom, you taught me that I had as good or better chance as anyone.
You taught me of Love, understanding, and are my best friend!
Please! <u>I don't want you to end!!!</u>
You caught my every tear, and gave the best hugs.
And made me believe that I was better than all those thugs.
With all my wrongs that I do and did you never saw them,
or at least kept it very well hid.
The Love you gave to me was second only to <u>God!</u>
You had all that Love for the boy who was so odd!
I finely got a real mother but, I didn't know she was only to lend.
<u>Mommy! I don't want you to end!!!</u>
Forgive me for all those times I hurt you, in that very special part.
<u>Oh yes, I do know how many times I had broken your heart.</u>
In my whole life there was one funereal I never thought I would have to attend.
<u>Please mom, I don't want to see you end!!!</u>
Dear sweet God, don't send her to her death!
For I will gladly <u>give you my very last breath!!!</u>
I do know everything happens the way you see fit.
But please, I beg of you to make this ligate.
My very soul to you I will send.
<u>Let my moms heart know, I don't want to see you end!!!</u>

By
Billy

Flame!🌹👤☺

Danielle Knew

Danielle was no secret; she had plans all the way.
And given the right person, she knew just what to say.
She was not as people saw her, not at all.
There were so many times we wanted to say to you these cards
To you were still dealt.
Never for you was a great hand.
But graceful as you were taught it just happens to be what you got.
There's something you saw without a doubt
I hate to say this but this is what you were a bout.
We have not seen the last of that is no doubt!
We all know that you are far away as a shout!
We can all kid ourselves, but everything said here is something that we must do.
Kind of like Danielle knew!

By
Flame

Flame!

Deceit

All my life I was told to watch out.
Don't ever, trust people there is always
a doubt.
Trust is not a game very easily plaid.
And the thought of it can always fade.
Read the book until it is complete.
And find out just what becomes of deceit!
Truth is always great, so, yes it is the key.
No, deceit will never set you free.
If your feet are really planted in the concrete.
Nothing, will cause you to retreat.
If you falter now and then.
Say your prayers and don't do them again.
Remember this, there's only one that
holds the receipt.
And there's only one choice, stay away from
Deceit!

By
Flame

Flame!🌹☺

Experience of the Heart

A tender touch, just so you know.
I simply have nowhere else to go.
Times are short I have to say.
Just listen, jump on that day.
Let's get past the game that's hurting us all.
And hang together and have a great ball.
Just remember from you I will not part.
Famished, I will not eat you alive.
Just don't let the horse before the kart.
For this is Experience of the heart
don't let somebody say, truly is the way.
This is where my humble heart stays.
Forgive me if I experienced something so new.
Here is something I should tell all of you.
There is something that makes me stop and feel.
That life is good no matter how feel.
There is something in life that makes me understand.
I must have known all the way back from the start.
And it really tears me apart.

By
Flame

Flame!

Echoes of the Heart

You say I am a genius and that's ok.
Truly that does not destroy my day.
And it does not pull me a part.
For truly, it is the echoes of the heart.
There was a game that we played so well.
But there was a time, that we forgot,
one time we fell.
And we never got to fare with that.
I really don't want to go to
where that's at.
And life will set you right at the start.
But all I feel is the echoes of the heart.
But can you give me what is
real and straight.
Because life has way to much hate.
Give me something so real.
Let me have something to feel.
Give me a place where I can start.
Because I need to feel the echoes
of the heart!

By
Flame

Flame!🌹😊

Flame Never Forgot

Faces have blurred, and names there were a lot.
But the absurd thing is, Flame never forgot!
Rains come and go but something's remain.
They say he's crazy as for me, I think he is absolutely sane.
He can be a handful, but his memory always stays true.
Trust me, chances are he has not forgotten you.
Giving the most he can for your very soul.
Maybe he is crazy, because it seems that is his only goal.
Tears of happiness running down your face.
To make you feel good that's what it takes.
So next time you're feeling warm and it's getting kind of hot.
Have no worries, and know Flame never forgot!
To him, for you there could be no pain at all.
For you, He would defiantly take a fall.
He is always a friend and his friendship begot.
But Flame never forgot!
I am with you and will never leave your side.
You are my one and only pride.
Until death takes me and my guts start to rot.
You are in my heart, because Flame never forgot!

By
Flame

Flame!

Fraudulent

I sit back and watch people do their thing.
I see the cowardly I see the strength and have
kneeled before a king.
I've also spent time in places kind of convent.
But the one thing I've never been fraudulent.
I got your back, wherever you go.
You are the reality of my world.
So please baby don't cut the cord.
I want you to know I really have not one complaint.
But I happen to know, that the good Lord sent to Angels
to bring us here.
You make me feel good inside truly your tolerant.
But I can see in your eyes that you are not fraudulent.

By
Flame

Flame!🌹☺

My Mother

Mom, you were always tough right from the start.
But, you always gave me all the love in your heart.
And all the wisdom you've had throughout the years.
Is truly the only reason that I am here!
There where so many times when I just didn't understand.
So you told me, when to love and when to stand.
I am the baby of three great brothers.
And this must be true, because they came
from my mother.
Mom, when I am not near I still think highly of you!
But every time I look into your eyes I still see truth.
I just want you to know, I think of you
both day and night.
Please know I hold you close to my heart, and how you taught me wrong from right.
Understand mom, I only wish for a little sunshine for you in each passing day.
But if things ever get a little bit dark?
Remember, you have established an awful lot of love for you here in my heart!
As for me, you taught me that fighters fight, and you gave birth to a champ!
I might be self-taught but I was never a tramp.
So let me knock this out and say, I am different, from all the others.
Because I come from the greatest!!! My mother!!!

By
Flame
(Billy)

Hurt You

I love you more and more since the day we met.
A gambler would say that for me you are
my best bet.
But it seems that you would like to renounce me
from your love.
And I always felt as if we were like the hand
and the glove.
I filled your space and your warmth kept us
right on Q.
But I must be crazy, because I hurt you.
Now I cry all day, and at night you never
leave my sleep.
My heart and soul I truly want you to keep!
Can't you even begin to look inside of me?
Because if you could, I just know that
you would see.
That within me there is no deceit.
Please, let's get down to the real truth.
Never again will I let myself, or anyone,
Hurt you!

By
Flame

Flame!☙☺

Going Down

I am a man of peace and love but I have been captured.
Not to bring myself up, but I am a man of rapture.
Not to say that, I've done nothing wrong in this town.
But I'm not the man that's going down.
My feet are planted firmly and I'm doing so well.
My life is a paradise I see no hell.
I have touched the cloth that is why and only he wears.
I only listen to what he says, for it is only fair.
As people look at the grass, I only see the blade
beneath my feet.
Truly I say to you, my heart will not skip a beat.
Heaven is the place I will always be found.
So listen when I say, I'm a man who's not going down.
Am I crazy for thinking this way?
I think not, and this is what I have to say.
I fought with the devil and knocked him around.
Yes, this is one man that is not going down.
Eternity, is the view I have, now stop right there
and don't you laugh.
Let me explain to you exactly what have.
I am the pure snowflake that falls from the sky.
I am the truth amongst all the lies.
So when you meet me have some taste.
Just shake my hand, and remember God doesn't make waste.
Yes, my hands will never be bound.
And this man is not going down!

By
Flame

Flame!☙☺

Help You Hold On

I see the tear in your eyes.
And you feel like you can touch
the cascading skies.
You would give it all back to see the
Night mares all be gone.
Feel my heart, and know, I will help you hold on.
I want to hold you just like a rose.
I take you like medicine, but with you
there is no normal dose.
There once was a movie beauty and the beast.
I can feel the honesty at the very least.
The forgotten heart is lonely at best.
Trying to figure out when you had that zest.
Gone are the days you can turn every head.
And living is not easy when you have no bread.
I always picture you barefoot standing
on the lawn.
I feel you're every shiver as I help you hold on.
A child with in you, is something that I have seen.
And you have known about this, back
when you were a teen.
One day I told you something when
it was just about dawn.
I think it went something like this, so just remember I will help you hold on.

By
Flame

Flame!❀ɞ☺

I Have Hope

Something is wrong but, they gave me hope.
Some say I am crazy, some say, I am on dope.
It is so insane what they will do.
The things they say are so untrue.
The ventures they want to take.
From this dream I wish they would a wake.
If the devil ties me up with rope.
He would lose again, because I have hope.
I can say that I have walked on
the edge of resistance.
And I don't believe there is a remittance.
I believe there is nothing wrong with the scroll.
Say what you will, I will pay that toll.
I am a firm believer, don't you know?
And I am a man that will continue to grow.
There is always something out there
and I have hope.
Times are hard and that's everywhere you go.
Remember what you reap, so that is
what you will sew.
Respect is an easy word to say, but the actions
are hard to do.
So remember we are not under the telescope.
And I tell you I have hope!

By
    Flame

Flame! ☺

I know I will be okay

Life is good so they say.
But, I will do okay.
Dropped out of nowhere, there are Crimes in the streets.
But I also understand, I am just another viewer of the things
they say are concrete.
I'm just a child; I love my family, friends, and the people I meet.
I'm just a little girl with a lot to do.
No one can tell I might be something strong for you.
You might think what good can this child do for me?
But mommy, I'm telling you to try to understand.
Give me the strength to make you understand.
I give you my love without remorse.
Just to let us both understand of course.
Today is my birthday I have to say I'm glad.
My circle of family and friends thought well.
That's something with you I don't think I have to tell.
From a child's heart, this is all I got to say.
Don't worry mommy, I know I will be okay!

By
Flame

Flame! 🌹☺

I Love This

This woman has fallen down
She was hurt once, and lost her crown.
Her dress was torn just like her heart.
And this was only the very start.
I live my life one day at a time.
But in her eyes I seemed to have found a sign.
Gifted in so many ways I really could tell.
I tried to pick her up and clean her off well.
She reached up and gave me the sweetest kiss.
And all I could think of was, I love this.
Given so much freedom in ways that
I cannot comprehend.
I can feel the honesty of the truth she sends.
Hand in hand we go through life like this.
Being with her in so many ways feels like bliss.
I treat her like a rose that never was picked.
And all the while I feel she needs to be fixed.
She is a fantasy that has come true.
And there are times I really don't know
what to do.
So I will just say it, just what it is.
When it comes to her really I just love this.

By
Flame

Flame! ☺

I Saw Mom Best

I said to my brother not to long ago.
I want so bad to see mom, so bad before she goes!
And I pulled up a file from my mind.
So with that I realized she never did leave me behind.
The gifts she gave to me, were great at the very least.
Gave me three angels to keep me from that beast!
Pete, Larry, and George had taught me right from the start.
That my mom always had me in her heart!!!
Strength is within not without.
And through her, they showed what that was all about.
My mom took me to a place so high, that I would never had fear!
And now that she is no longer here.
I think somehow she knows, she taught me well that my own life I can steer.
And for this I can attest.
Truly, I saw mom best!!!

By
Flame

Flame!🌹☺

I Shall Finish The Game!

Here is your first clue, listen to purple rain.
Only then will you see this, I shall finish the game!
Brought up to be a spiritual man.
I dare to love the very best I can.
With no doubts I have always been the same.
So please face me as I say, I shall finish the game!
So now I am treading all this water.
I just cannot get any hotter.
As I look into my father's eyes.
I comprehend that his presents will remain.
So please understand, I shall finish the game!
But, I do know that you have led me to this place.
And I see all the terror you try to hide upon your face.
Yes, I see that love, that use to be there in your heart.
Truest me when I say I haven't lost you, not that part.
When I have seen the last of the light within your eyes.
Both of us together, with the angels we will fly.
So no matter, whether you feel I am right or totally insane.
Remember this, my tender one, I shall finish the game!

By
Flame

Flame!❦☺

If You only Knew

My heart was yours at hello.
You had me every sense don't you know.
Your succulent ways caught me at the start.
Your thoughts were genuine and
you're pretty smart.
It would be desolate without you in my life.
And you're sensational with your love
as my wife.
This description can only be about you.
You unraveled my world, if you only knew?
You are my sexual fantasy I must say.
And through my eyes you always will
be this way.
You are my hope, and you are my dreams.
With you by my side I can conquer all things.
When I touch you I start to shiver and shake.
The beauty within you is almost too hard to take.
And with you I just can't be fake.
I would kill or die for you, that is the truth.
Sweetheart, if you only knew?
I suffer with pain every time you walk out the door.
Every time you leave my heart has another sore.
My soul is yours to take and command.
You can make me do anything with a touch of your hand.
Since I met you, my love for you only grew.
Oh my sweetness if you only knew?

By
Flame

Flame!☙☺

– 45 –

Lost!

I was born within a bitter frost.
But you know, I seemed to have quickly gotten lost.
My early childhood, I found myself in such great pain.
And last night I had that nightmare again.
It seems that it just won't ever go away.
I have no choice, it comes back every day.
My mind, my heart, and every bit of my soul.
The bustard took me down, he took all
of me so cold.
I am told to not think about it, it's all in the past.
Remember all those good things that were a blast.
So I say, but I did pay for everything and at such a cost.
And now my whole life is lost.
She brought me back to the man I use to be.
And so I feel once again that chilling frost
coming onto me.
Will she love me right till the end.
Or is she a far wither friend.
That love that she offers is nothing but for her.
And yet, there is something I try to deter.
There is nothing and absolutely at any coast.
I wouldn't pay to not be lost.
But, she is gone as she gives my heart a toss.
And here I sit totally lost!

By
Flame

Flame! ☺

My Heart Died

Have you ever seen a heart bleed?
You know as if it was hurt from doing a good deed.
Well, a young woman took me for a great ride.
And when she was through my heart died.
I have not seen beauty such as this ever that I know.
I just had to see this through and watch her grow.
All I knew is this was a great honor, and I really tried.
But, yes in the end my heart died!
Life had not begun yet, at least not for me.
I was off in a tangent to set this woman free.
In no way would she know what she's got.
Hard as I tried she could not be taught.
So as she laughed while I cried.
That was the day my heart died.

By
Flame

Flame!☺

Once

He fell to pieces and struggled his way through.
He's had a very hard life this is true.
In the shell of this temple, a man
Just wanted to grow.
There was nothing that he did not want to know.
He was not dumb or even close to a dunce.
He was loving and kind until this once!
Here comes that old broken heart.
The love was not there, and
his knowledge fell apart.
Taken for granite that he could think
through it all.
This is what brought on the big fall.
Now all alone, the bed is half full.
And the nights are empty and that's no bull.
He has experienced something that does taunt.
For the rest of his life, this will haunt!
And for the rest of his days he will
only answer in grunts.
Only because she took his heart that once!
All the dreams have stopped but,
the nightmares continue.
He continues to cry because he does not
recognize what is true.
God help this man we all pray for him.
Do not let this prosiest for his eyes grow dim.
And all he knows is he has been deceived.
If she only knew that in her, he always believed.
Yes his wife was she, so he gave his love to her in abundance.
So, that other love, she went to really
pulled some stunts.
A tear will always fall from his eye, all because she broke him down that Once!

By
Flame

Flame!

I Wish

I wish there was a way I could count all the stars.
I wish I was the one that invented cars.
I wish she had believed me when I said I loved her.
I wish I was young, and age did not have to occur.
I wish old was something new.
I wish my mistakes were so few.
I wish I did not dream of death every night.
I wish I had the nerve to fight.
I wish to go to heaven every day.
I wish I could see everyone; I have so much to say.
I wish I never really did hurt you.
I wish I knew for sure that you were true.
I guess I'm never going to have that dish.
You know what?
I wish!

By
Flame

Flame!

I agree

Miracles happen this I know.
Dazzling and sweet this is how it goes.
We've all been there we've all seen it is true.
But just like karma does it will come back to you.
Shaking the universe and rocking the earth.
Dammit! Don't you see what you're worth?
Not what you see is what you visualize with such ease.
And with that little bit of information I agree!
And when you take two lovers that think the
other is appealing.
But they just won't let their heart start feeling.
With a cool summer breeze and a nice cup of tea.
So bring out the good and dissipate the bad for these
things I agree!
A weeping willow has the strength to bend; we should be as strong as that tree.
Please understand, for this I agree!
Then our lives are spent to get to death in the end.
Simple directions to that point still we think
we have to defend.
Life wasn't meant to be easy or hard.
Sometimes all we can do is pray for the next best card.
And I find in the saying the best things in life are free.
Yes it's true, damn I agree!

By
Flame

Flame!🌹👁☺

I Do Feel

Certainly I have come to this decision.
It comes to me in such a vision.
Mass confusion will come up on us as a thief.
Suddenly I understand the phrase, turn
over a new leaf.
We have all heard about the secret seal.
Well, it has already been broken, truly I do feel.
It is all coming true, please let me explain.
The goodies always, come last, so first
we must feel the pain.
There are people that think my world is not real.
But faith takes me to a place that I do feel.
That discretion is used, to make our wrongs right.
Compromised so much that we lose our site.
The body and blood with a map that shows
us the right road.
That leads us to the land of milk, honey and gold.
Running around with fear that comes
from deep within.
How far must we go before we see that sin.
Please, allow me to tell you the deal.
The elders are the ones we need to trust I do feel.
There is only one choice and that is to converse.
Before we are deleted and carried a
way in a hares.
I know you've heard life is a drop in the ocean.
And I have to say I second that notion.

Cont.

(2)

We all are running around as if the answers cannot be found.
And I think it's time for us to find solid ground.
It's your heart, it's something we cannot steal.
It's forgiveness; yes that's what I do feel.
Majestic is something that we all want to be.
But to be humble, faithful, and loyal
can make us free!
It is crazy what goes through our head.
From the moment we are born till the day
we are dead.
A lie has become a convenience it really seems.
We cannot afford to let this happen not
even in our dreams.
Our emotions are strong, our minds are quick, and our hearts will reveal.
This crazy thing called love honestly I do feel.
So be not lost by what you hear or what you think.
But just know that each one of us is a link.
There is not one I have met that does not
need to heal.
So just look to God, and know, that this I do feel.

By
Flame

Flame!🥀☺

Really I don't know

She really knows me what can I say.
And she was always there back in the day.
Running away from my side, yet telling me that I was her pride.
Running with her, in the streets that
led to the ability.
Is she crazy and on the go.
My sweet friend I really don't know.
I can conceive that we are great friends.
I just don't know, if she believes that I will be there until the end.
But it is my strongest hope our friendship
and love will grow.
Alas I reckon I really don't know.
She likes to keep me on my feet.
Power and prestige probably she just can't see.
Rolling with the thunder and the lightning just dazzles her smile.
But you know, for her, I would walk that last mile.
I would fight any heathen, and destroy any troll.
Would she do the same for me? With tears,
I say that I really don't know.
She is so unsure of my love, I just want
this lady to understand.
That life is like a river and there are times when
we all need a hand.
Surely this woman is in my soul.
Under certain situations truly I feel, I am not her foe.
I can be whatever she likes, but to her it's not true so, I just really don't know.

By
Flame

Flame!❦☺

It's Time!

Let me try to give you a revelation.
Truly this is the situation.
Let it be known, my intelligence is not that great.
But I need to tell you about one man's fate.
There is a metamorphosis I've been going through.
I can no longer keep away the truth!
You see, since a child I was being prepared.
For being a man that his soul would be bared.
IT'S TIME!
In quantum physics, the possibilities are
endless please understand.
The present is all I can see.
For now, pain is all I get to see!
The love in one man's heart is not big enough.
With a gentle soul I have learned to be tough.
The grace I have felt in so many others.
And way too many people hide under the covers.
Metaphorically I could stop it on the dime.
But reality says IT'S TIME!

Cont.

(2)

Something was making my heart cold.
Yes, wisdom I had to learn as I got old.
And to the people, who say I am demonic, let's get this
out of the way!
This is not at all, what I have say.
Pushing me away would only be a crime.
Clearly I say to you, IT'S TIME!
Growing up I had this thought of doing something good.
Never having the thought that someday I would.
Within me there is a realm that has no end.
While looking at this, I think there is no such thing as a friend.
But please understand, there is no remorse coming from me.
There truly is an ore that surrounds my every being.
So listen, I am the one that does the healing.
I will not be, just the one to make the Rime.
So please remember this.
IT'S TIME!!!!

By
Flame

Flame!

Just a Glance

I pride myself on romance.
For this is what I've seen of my LIFE just A GLANCE!
I have seen it all is not a painting, OR A MURAL on the wall.
I have to say given some chance.
I saw it all, in A glance!
There's nothing I wouldn't do for you on this day.
Other than try to understand you love me this Way.
I did not see this coming, please try to understand.
Go away and leave me alone.
Don let me give you this alone.
The Rocks I give away but the pebbles I seem to keep.
For these, are the sins that I reap.
Go away and say there is no more.
Just tell me what it's about just say what for.
I have gotten no so much more about what you do.
Sweetheart I can't say enough, I love you.
Shut down my shaft.
Just call me a raft.

Cont.

(2)

Just let me be your Savior and I'll be just that.
I'm not trying to suck you dry or anything like that.
But I will pull out a few rabbits out of my hat.
I've never had anybody believe in me why don't you?
I understand the sucking of a man close to you.
Is this the way you would treat anybody and is this what you do?
Forgive me your hardship owner.
Should I play it smooth or did I win you over?
Did I cover you or not, or did I Carrie you on my shoulder.
If it was up to me you would have no snow.
Just let me be I will be okay.
Just remember when I say.
Allow me to be yours if that's okay.
Give development to me.
And I have the love of a mother and father and his son.
Never let it go unknown right up to this day.
Baby I am begging you.
To truly seeping through.
I'm just asking you please?
Just saying your walking around in your underpants.
I really haven't given you the chance.
To allow me to see you,
at a glance!

By
Flame

Flame!🌹☺

Just a thought

You walked into my life and threw me into a daze.
And every sense then I have has been some kind of haze.
Forget me you, and all that happens.
When it comes down to it, I reckon neither one
of us are captains.
And it really doesn't matter to me how many times we fought.
Just don't let your heart turn into the thought.
I like nature it comes natural to me.
Please understand, in you this is what I see
my heart pounds genuinely for you.
Please understand this baby, there's nothing I wouldn't do for you.
To be forgiven for the things I will not ask.
For my sweetness, this is my life time task.
If there is anything in this world for you that I have bought.
Since I've chased you my love is what you caught.
So ignorant as I am please, believe this about you
I thought!

By
Flame

Flame!🌹😊

Just Listen

You brought my heart back to life with your smile and the way your eyes glisten.
You and I have something together, please just listen.
Once I was a man, bold, and proud of yourself.
But now I feel it's all about the wealth.
Together I just know that we can see spectacular views.
And to this day I feel we have all the right moves.
Shared thoughts, dreams, hopes, I don't believe
I have to say.
You have been extraordinary from that very first day.
But somehow I feel between the two of us we
must make a revision.
So, my sweetness please listen.
Devastation may come upon world.
And at times we will feel that into another place
we've been hurled.
But don't give up on the love that has been
handed to you.
All the stares are lit up in the sky.
They are all for you, I do not tell a lie.
Your beauty is unimaginable please try to understand.
I just want to be you're everything, not just you're man.
Just give me a chance to prove this to you because,
I know I will.
I do not have a forked tongue and I am not hessian.
Just feel your heart, and try hard to just listen.

By
Flame

Flame!🥀👁☺

– 59 –

Life Encumbers Death

Here it comes night splitting into the day.
We really don't understand it, it's just the way.
Given each day, we can assume it's there.
Nobody said that's fare.
I have seen this in breathing my breath.
And so I say, life encumbers death.
Help us all, whatever you are and may be.
We're all grateful trust us with what we see.
Depression is how we carry on, please understand.
All we want is a helping hand.
Somehow we feel we are great.
We're flying so high with our mental state.
Seriously is there a doubt in your head.
In the mornings do you make your bed?
I'm not trying to see anything less.
Just allow me to say life encumbers death.
See it upside down if you like, surely you will be right on time.
And for me to get to your soul is right on the dime.
If you're soul goes astray for any length of time.
Trust me, all hell will break loose.
And set before you there will be no excuse.
Given all of this I am sure you can not
turn the dial.

Con't

(2)

I am the Flame, telling you what to do.
From here on in, you will only here the truth.
Gravity, will pull you in another direction.
But only if you have the strength to hang on to that section.
It started off as the wall.
Our eyes are now open so hear your call.
Here we go, were going to take that dive.
Hop in the bus and when we say this thing, God we are alive.
So let me tell you what I have heard.
I have heard of this through the song of a bird.
And it captured my every word.
There is nothing that ever took my breath.
When I finely learned that life encumbers death!

By
Flame

Flame!

Lost Me

Here I sit, so simple and wise.
Believe it or not, I'm a small package with a great big size.
I've been beat to hell by so many men.
Each and every time saying it won't happen again.
My life went blank and always has been.
It's not about what you've got it's about what you can give.
So you can heed to my word and start to live.
Okay, then just draw your mighty sword.
I thought such words kept me free.
But truly that's what has lost me.
Don't flash around like you see something I don't.
You know, I had chances to be what I wanted to be.
All I can say, is you lost me?

By
Flame

Flame!🥀😊

My Delight

It came to me on the day we met.
Most people would say it was off set.
It's just something else on the shelf that gets played with then gets put back.
I thought I had this love in the sack.
Determination is what they say it takes.
But you never know who the players might attack.
But I knew right away from the first night.
That truly, God gave me my delight.
Through most of my life I have learned that not too many know the rules.
But now I know what they mean by these fools.
I couldn't have dreamed of anything better.
Then going through everything with her and
in all kinds of weather.
So I will spend my life trying to give my
wife the very best!
No matter how many times I've got to pass the test.
Surely I will never give up on her and never
give up completely.
Because I believe in what my heart sees freely.
It's only for her that I see in the real light.
That she brings it right to my soul and shows me,
my delight!

By
Flame

Flame! 🙂

Help me Mend

I have been broken in so many ways.
For so long, I can't count the days.
I tried so hard, all the rules I couldn't bend.
I need that love to help me mend.
I know I have skinned my knees trying to
hold on to my love.
So I prayed to God up above.
Is there anyone that you could please send?
Sweet Lord, help me mend.
Caught up within all this catastrophe.
It's like an ocean of misery.
My heart has fallen into this oh so deep.
Into my soul, the craziness it seems to creep.
I have prayed all my life to get what I feel I need.
For this woman id hope you had planted a seed.
I blame her for hurting me the way she does.
I no longer can remember trust and love.
Give me the power to say I am.
she needs me, damn!
Is there anything that you can recommend?
As I start Crying out my last tear,
I ask help me mend.

By
Flame

Flame!🌹☺

No Doubt Here

I hold a prayer in my heart for God.
Give on to me, strong like a rod.
This was the prayer of a young man in such need.
He was so sure, that this prayer would
help him succeed.
But of course, he was in such pain he had his
doubts about this.
And there was a woman that loved him from
the first kiss.
He had always thought that God would
hear his request.
As time passed him by he wondered why.
Don't you hear me God? Aren't you the father
beyond the sky?
It has been 40 years, and the man
prayed every day.
So God put him on his knees and said, let me dry your tear.
I am Alfa and Omega and there is no doubt here.
Impatiently you have waited for this thing.
My child, I am all knowing, I see that
which you cannot.
I sent you down another road because I know best, or my child, have you forgot.
So my child, please give me all you care about.
Because my sweetest one,
there is no doubt!

By
Flame

A chance

I just wanted to grow,
wasn't trying to hurt anyone bro.
Only wanted to be the one with all the romance!
So here I sit ready to take a chance.
Honor justice truth are awaiting to be
loosened upon us right now.
People ask me all the time.
Are you in your prime?
The existing I've always wanted to know.
So listen here we go.
So this we shall enhance.
I beg of you let's take a chance.

By
Flame

Flame!🌹☺

Cowboy up

Cowboy up that's what I see.
The dress code is not what you see, but the truth is what you see in me!
Give me a day give me a night truly I will show you what's wrong and right
I truly live in my cynical ways.
But to be wrong with you is absolutely out of my mind.
I'm not a one want to be I'm not anything at all
just listen to my words and you might see
peace love care are all suitable word.
If I dressed the way that you want
throughout my life will you hunt.
So let my say a cool would that people say sup.
However I say Lets Cowboy up!

By
Flame

Just One Day

I have had enough, it's getting pretty bad!
But they all say the same, please don't feel so bad.
I feel I have been thrown in some place that I didn't want to be.
So people try to make me feel, guilty as if.
I was created special, and like I have
this great gift.
I cannot come close to that, there is no way.
I am so sad, I would give up every year of my life. For
no tears not one, and no more strife.
Tapered honesty drips down my face.
Lost lovers that cannot be replaced.
Encumbered friendships that are broke in two.
What is more important, I truly ask you!
Addicted, to life's little games.
After all, aren't we all quickly trained?
I have been realizing all these things this way.
So I have only one prayer and,
that is to understand,
just one day!

By
Flame

Flame!☺

Oh So Sad

I've been waiting for that special woman
to come by.
Looks like I shall search for her to the
end of my days, I tell no lie.
I am not here to make anyone feel bad.
And yet it is relentless don't you think.
Honest this is not some sort of fade.
Just to gaze upon her makes me feel so glad.
But like many, I say oh so sad.
All I have is a chance to show her who I really am.
I don't want to be like a wolf next to this lamb.
But let me tell you the truth of it all.
For her, I have had my back against the wall.
She is like a gentle breeze; a fresh sent I have never had.
And yet sometimes, it is oh so sad.
She's like that dream you know, that one that
always gets a way.
But, if she's ever captured, it will have
been done in vain.
I would give her anything, everything she wanted,
and all those things that she never had.
With you I could never ever be oh so sad.

By
Flame

Flame! 🌿☺

So Divine

I once met a man with a heart of gold.
He taught me that I can have peace in my soul.
It was strange really to me.
The unusual things that, he could only see.
A holy man he was I felt.
It seems to me he could handle any hand he was dealt.
It was almost as if he were some kind of sign.
He was so divine.
Cut from all of it he seemed to survive.
And his eyes were never dim, they were so much alive.
Yes as far as I could see this man walked a straight line.
He was so divine.
And in that golden moment I was able
to catch a glimpse.
Suddenly I felt as if I had to submit.
Like an old glove that just seemed to fit.
He never spoke to repeat a line.
He was so divine.
Let me go and just try to ponder.
What it is you want me conjure?
He spoke in a gentle whisper with me.

By
Flame

Flame!☺

Please stop!

Don't give me any of your bullshit, and don't give me
any of your lines.
Help me understand you or what's left.
You are beautiful in every damn way.
Assume it is possible I am this way.
Give me something to work with not just a harebrained idea.
No matter what I can do I will find something higher.
I don't know what you went through I could really care less.
If there was a way you went through, I have been there
I must confess.
Jack Ripper and all those guys, I care less than them
then anything in the world.
If this is the way you were brought up to love and all of this.
Tell me something has it always been with such ease.
Well my dearest sweetheart let me tell you this for free.
STOP IT PLEASE!!!

By
Flame

The moon was on fire.

Shivers up my spine and raises the hairs on my neck.
But there are some things we don't wreck-a-lect.
I study your smoothness and all of your sensation.
I have to say truly, you are the best of my generation.
Your gracefulness is all I desire.
I knew the first time we slid into each other.
It was like lightning bolts and crackling thunder.
Something about your eyes, they put me in a trance.
You were so comfortable this was
the greatest romance.
Taking on the world so great and being so strong!
It was an ore about you that just dazzled me.
I once was a bum but then became a sire.
Baby, I knew the moon was on fire.
As soon as you touched me my heart started to fluster.
Just like that movie Billy and Buster.
Let me lay it on the line Just the way I always do.
I look into your eyes, I only since the truth.
And the glory of all is you are truly my one desire.
Yes my sweetness, I felt you, and the moon was on fire!

By
Flame

Flame! ☺

Disarrayed

There came a day in my life when I had prayed.
Lord, forgive me but I am so disarrayed!
Please don't forsake me, since a child I have had
Faith in you.
Just lead me on and tell me what to do.
Just a little help and, I will not be the one that strayed.
Please take a way this feeling of being disarrayed!
Set my soul on fire and take this beast away from me.
God, allow me to be your slave so that I can be free.
I thought I had this whole thing mapped out, but that's when I became afraid.
And ever since then I have been disarrayed!
There is also the fact that I long for you to be everywhere I go.
And I know you saw every game I ever played.
So hear my cry, and please take away this
feeling of disarrayed!

By
Flame

The Shell in a Pine Box

A wasted life they all thought I had.
As for me, I did not think it was half bad.
They called me a doormat, someone to
be disposed of.
Never knowing that, I had an abundance of love.
And in my time, thrown at me, there
where many rocks.
So my heart breaks for those who can only see
the shell in a pine box.
And for eons this phrase shall stand.
Although, I was not god, I was simply a man.
I was not special, or above the others.
But yes, I have a secret for my brothers.
Just forget about it, it is all coming to an end so, don't bother to look at your clocks.
And remember the shell in a box!
I give all my love to each one of you people.
So make sure your tears fill that steeple.
And as you walk away, and act as dumb as a fox.
Just tell each other how you felt love coming from,
the shell in the box.

By
Flame

Flame!❀ʓ☺

Left Behind

A thought occurred to me and it was a great big sign.
It is not that people leave us yet were left behind.
We cry and we weep for the ones that have left us.
However in my mind this is nothing more than mistrust.
Lo and behold it is a great thing to leave this earth.
In all that we have done here shows our worth.
It's a given thing all that we do.
Forgive me for saying so but I lie not to you.
But I think if you search hard enough you will find.
It's truly a hardship to be left behind!
I truly hope there is some truth in what I say.
As a spiritual man I can only tell you in God obey!
His word is 1st his word is the last his word is forever!
So if you think differently let me tell you that is when you and
him are severed!
So when you think of your loved ones who leave this earth.
Don't think of their passing think of their worth.
And if any of you read this poem I hope you will find.
Just remember where the ones left behind!!!

By
Flame

Flame!🌿☺

Love Me

In my mind I have no harm for you don't you see.
So I can't understand in my mind why you can't love me.
My heart is bigger than most, smaller than many others.
I've always thought that we should stick together just like brothers.
My teardrops fall and hit the ground just like rain.
The hurt in this world can truly drive me insane.
I've always been told you can't give away what you don't have.
So is it so hard to borrow something to give to someone and
see them a laugh.
Most people don't know the show is never over until they see.
I'm not looking for a standing ovation just love me.
I understand love can be painful and many ways.
And yet sometimes it's the warmth of a sunny day.
All too often our hearts break in many pieces.
And many times it's just fake and just teases.
Emotions will get the better of us if we are not in total control.
With the exception of love that should be our goal.
I asked give you only one thing as you can see.
Love me!

By
Flame

Flame!☺

It's Time!

Let me try to give you a revelation.
Truly this is the situation.
Let it be known, my intelligence is not that great.
But i need to tell you about one man's fate.
There is a metamorphosis I've been going through.
I can no longer keep away the truth!
You see, since a child i was being prepared.
For being a man that his soul would be bared.
It's time!
In quantum physics, the possibilities are
endless please understand.
The present is all i can see.
For now, pain is all i get to see!
The love in one man's heart is not big enough.
With a gentle soul i have learned to be tough.
The grace i have felt in so many others.
And way too many people hide under the covers.
Metaphorically i could stop it on the dime.
But reality says it's time!
Something was making my heart cold.
Yes, wisdom i had to learn as i got old.
and to the people who say i am demonic, let's get this
Out of the way!

Con't

(2)

This is not at all, what i have said.
Pushing me away would only be a crime.
Clearly i say to you, it's time!
Growing up i had this thought of doing something good.
Never having the thought that someday i would.
Within me there is a realm that has no end.
While looking at this, i think there is no such thing as a friend.
But please understand, there is no remorse coming from me.
There truly is an ore that surrounds my every being.
So listen, i am the one that does the healing.
I will not be, just the one to make the rime.
So please remember this.
It's time!!!!

By
Flame

Flame!🌹☺

Do What You Got To Do

Do what you got to do!
It's really okay if you feel you have to do what you do.
I have been a merchant for many years.
I have cried my share of tears.
I am not as smart as you think I am.
However, I'm just a man.
Just let me go insane with what I thought.
Do not let me forget what I thought.
Give me the privilege of seeing you through.
Swear to God, this is all I want do.
However to bring me to this point,
here I am to anoint.
I will take my last breath for you.
No joke this is what I would do.
With all the medications that I take, let me say.
I May have to take off this attitude that can't be counted.
So I can truly be mounted.
Truly I am not conceded.
But, I am distilled, and I have not been receded.
Give me the chance to prove to him right, so give me the
gift of sight.

Con't

(2)

I know you're smarter than me I cannot count the times.
I was taught as child, that things go right.
But will that happen tonight.
So don't play me as some kind of fool.
I am not that person you think and that's so cruel.
If, you believe in me that's just fine.
Just understand I have been there so many times.
I do have lots of goodness inside me.
Just give me a place, where I know what I should be.
Just let me know where I stand.
God. Let me be my own man.
If I have not lived up to your expectations, up until now.
Maybe you can help me, with that somehow.
Give me my life, or rather I have my death.
So let me say what I am trying to get out.
Just like you, I don't want to be a fool.
So in my mind, you should do what you to going to do!
Please, just let me live.
Really, here is how it is supposed to go, for it is not reality we're
supposed to know
My last memory, was forgive me as I you taught me to do.
I've not done well with my life without you.
I never knew this, but you were just telling me do what you got to do!

By
Flame

Flame!☺

I can see

Give me a little bit and I start to shake.
Just give me a little bit that's all I will take.
Fearful and scared yes I am.
I only do what I can.
Forsaken I saw all my brothers.
There is no way I forgot the others.
Shoot out and carry on.
This could be wrong.
Would you help me over the stumbling block?
Is it time to wind the clock?
Just never thought I'd have to stop.
I must've gotten it from my pop.
Give me that me that which is lost.
And I know it will come to me as such a cost.
I guess it really has to be.
Only because I can see!

By
Flame

Flame!🌿☺

A Beautiful Mind

There is a man who thinks of love and kindness.
There is nothing about this man
that is besides this
Emotions cover him like a blanket.
And no one knows exile or how to take it.
And this is what I find.
It's truly a beautiful mind!
Music he writes and poems he sings.
He can truly do most anything.
There isn't anything that can hold him in a bind.
For he is truly a beautiful mind!
Give him his life or give him his death.
And for his cause I believe he'll
give his last breath.
I swear that I wouldn't give you a line.
This is a man with a beautiful mind!
Roses are the aroma he smells.
And he sees every that spear that falls.
This is not someone who is just kind.
This is a beautiful mind!

By
Flame

Flame!☺

I Do Feel

Certainly I have come to this decision.
It comes to me in such a vision.
Mass confusion will come up on us as a thief.
Suddenly I understand the phrase, turn
over a new leaf.
We have all heard about the secret seal.
Well, it has already been broken, truly I do feel.
It is all coming true, please let me explain.
The goodies always, come last, so first
we must feel the pain.
There are people that think my world is not real.
But faith takes me to a place that I do feel.
That discretion is used, to make our wrongs right.
Compromised so much that we lose our site.
The body and blood with a map that shows
us the right road.
That leads us to the land of milk, honey and gold.
Running around with fear that comes
from deep within.
How far must we go before we see that sin.
Please, allow me to tell you the deal.
The elders are the ones we need to trust I do feel.
There is only one choice and that is to converse.
Before we are deleted and carried a
way in a hares.

Con't

(2)

I know you've heard life is a drop in the ocean.
And I have to say I second that notion.
We all are running around as if the answers cannot be found.
And I think it's time for us to find solid ground.
It's your heart, it's something we cannot steal.
It's forgiveness, yes that's what I do feel.
Majestic is something that we all want to be.
But to be humble, faithful, and loyal
can make us free!
It is crazy what goes through our head.
From the moment we are born till the day
we are dead.
A lie has become a convenience it really seems.
We cannot afford to let this happen not
even in our dreams.
Our emotions are strong, our minds are quick, and our hearts will reveal.
This crazy thing called love honestly I do feel.
So be not lost by what you hear or what you think.
But just know that each one of us is a link.
There is not one I have met that does not
need to heal.
So just look to God, and know, that this I do feel.

By
Flame

Flame!🌹☺

A life time lie

They told me of love and showed me hate.
They asked me to believe and they took my faith.
Friendship was supposed to be lifelong.
But when you have nothing to offer, you find that is wrong.
People tell that truth should be the only way.
But you catch them in lies each and every day.
When people told me of truth i would get so high.
But now i find it a life time lie!
Care and concern are only things you give.
It's only fantasy to think this is how people live.
Truth is only a comfort zone that people use.
For when they hurt you or so you don't see the fuse.
Life is a torment that slowly goes by.
For i have learned that it's just a life time lie!
I know my heart is nothing but a trampoline.
There for others to tear down my esteem.
the reason i no longer have any dreams.
Is because what i think doesn't matter it seems.
One truth is, i have no more tears to cry.
For throughout my years it's been a life time lie!
There is no good, there is no bad at all.
There is no devil, there is no heavenly call.
Everything there is in this world is but a short sigh.
I tell you the truth when i say it's a life time lie!!!

By
Flame

Flame!☺

A New Birth

A glow about your skin and a gleam
in your eyes.
Hair like honey when the sun shines
from the skies.
A special smile that lights up the world.
Who could ever deny that you are such a wonderful girl.
Rose colored cheeks that brighten the day.
You're spectacular, what can I say.
A ring on your finger holds us together.
Nothing else in the world could feel any better.
Your skin has that sensuous scent.
It's almost like together we were meant.
One day I gently placed my hand on your stomach and moved it around.
Together we created a miracle and of course
it was bound.
We both know being a parent is so much worth.
And today we are going to have a new birth.

By
Flame

Flame! ☺

A Godparents Love

They take away from your eye a tear.
For they take away all your fears.
They watch you crawl, they watch you stand.
They watch you cry, and they listen
to your demands.
And out of all this stuff.
They show a Godparents Love!
If you take God out of Godparents it's so siren.
Because God is the supreme.
Godparents are called that for a reason!
Because when all is gone what do we believe in?
They also have it so rough.
Because no matter what, they have to show a Godparents Love!
How lucky are we?
That we get to meet people like these.
They take the time to show us life in their view.
And then allow us to choose what we want to do.
And now I know God blessed me from above.
With a <u>GOD PARENTS LOVE!!!</u>

By
Flame

Flame!❧☺

A Special Brother Like You!

We are not together, and yet, we are never too far.
I mean, if I could reach the universe I
would give you a star.
Yes growing up there was always something new.
But that's just the way it is when you have a
<u>Special Brother Like You!</u>
You put love in my heart and
broadened my mind.
You taught me, piece in the end is what I will find.
I know that you think when you speak, words, I hear very few.
But how could I <u>NOT</u> learn, from a
<u>Special Brother Like You!</u>
You always gave me the courage I had to have.
And when I wanted to cry, somehow you
made me laugh.
Big brother, for you I would lay down and die.
I love you, and I hope you know
that's the reason why.
When I'm in the ground, and the grass
is full of dew.
I truly hope our mother knows, she gave me a <u>Special Brother Like You!</u>

By
Flame

Flame!🥀☺

Song Poem

Do you wish things on me?
do you want me to remember when your grandfather died.
Or would you rather me fill you with lies.
Is there some way I could've helped you through.
Please tell me is there anything I could do.
There is nothing else that I can possibly see.
Do you wish things on me.
I have not gotten the jest of the yet.
But I am willing to bet.
There is really nothing left to see.
You do wish things on me.
Like a love that never was there.
Or a man that never really did care.
None of these will you get from me.
There's only one thing I see.
And that is you do wish things on me!
Given the thought that there was love.
Shot down in the dark I'm a dead man.
And all I can ever see.
Is that wish you had for me!

By
Flame

Flame!🌹☺

Hanging On To a Thread
Hoping It Won't Break

I don't know what people think of me.
I don't know what they see.
They think I have it all together.
But I'm just flying through the weather.
I really think that they are making a big mistake.
Because I'm just hanging on to a thread
hoping it won't break!
People see what I have and think I'm doing ok.
But if they would just listen to what I have to say.
Really, I've had just about all I can take.
I'm just hanging on to a thread hopping
it won't break!
And let me tell you that I am honestly for real.
But let me tell the whole deal.
Sometimes it feels like my whole world
is nothing but fake.
And I'm hanging on to a thread
hoping it won't break!

By
Flame

Flame! ☺

Jade

God answered the prayers the world had prayed.
For he sent unto us a young lady named Jade!
Despite what it is her eyes see.
She only finds the good in you and me.
She plays music just like a bird.
And she is just as grate at the written word.
Also the art she creates will never fade.
There is just something really special about Jade!
There is something about her that makes her free.
And yet, she never forgets to be a lady.
Yes in her eyes there is beauty in everything made.
So don't ever pass up the chance to meet Jade!
She did not come in this world at
random please understand.
She was picked right from Gods very hand.
She is worth more than any gold that was ever paid.
We are so happy to have this lady named Jade!

By
Flame

Flame! ☺

My Responsibility

I was touch by God at birth with a responsibility.
What I am about to say is nothing but pure reality.
Content, peace, love, happiness, and self worth.
For everything is my responsibility from birth.
I am never to be violent, hate, steal, or lie.
I am to have total understanding for everything before my eyes.
To take pain away from your soul.
And give you total peace and harmony is my goal.
When tears of sorrow run down your face.
It is my responsibility to bring you to a joyful place.
I am to have the solution to the problem that weighs you down.
I am to treat you as if you were wearing a crown.
My responsibility is an enormous thing.
I am to make sure every blade of grass is in form and every bird sings.
Yes heaven will be here on earth.
And this is my responsibility from birth.
I must learn your deepest thought.
And replace it with something that just can't be bought.
The hurt and sorrow that you really feel.
It's up to me to change that, and that's the deal.
My responsibility has nothing to do with me.
But it is to create a space where you could be free.
So all I ask is for you to pray for me to see the reality.
That everything in the whole universe,
Is My Responsibility!

By
Flame

Flame!☺

The Price to Know

Please try to understand the nature of the game.
Not one of us are different, we're all the same.
Some people are there, but they don't tend to show.
They've had their problems too,
but they have paid the price to know.
I mean, people don't always talk about the pain they felt.
Or their heart was broke so bad they thought they would melt.
They paid the price for life's little idiosyncrasies.
To get this knowledge, they had to pay these little fees.
I also know it seems like they see which way to go.
But you must remember they pay the price to know.
It's like climbing a mountain or hopping a fence.
It doesn't seem to matter until you've had the experience.
I don't believe people do well just to put on a show.
I believe these people pay the price to know.
So the next time you're depressed, confused or distraught.
Just think of all the knowledge you just bought.
And when this stuff happens all in a row.
Think, this is only happening for me to pay the price to know.

By
Flame

Flame!🌿☺

Time to Make My Bed!

The sun shines and the leaves start to change.
As the world starts to rearrange.
There's a crispness in the air.
And yet it seems so unfair.
And as we slowly move into winter ahead.
I think it's time to make my bed!
Snowflakes softly float gently into the yard.
It's almost unbelievable that this is my card.
And I just can't get it out of my head.
That maybe it's time to make my bed!
I am putting all my ducks in a row.
Because in these times you just never know.
Everything around us is nothing more,
than a hologram.
We all make our mark, from the great ones to the one on the lamb.
So today I say my prayers and break bread.
And also I know it's time to make my bed!

By
Flame

Flame!☺

Bleed

I take it straight to the top.
Here's my plan to make it stop.
I always try to look out for others.
I will starve to feed my brothers.
I am a totally different breed.
For you I will bleed!
I haven't done enough in my eyes.
To stop all the deceit and lies.
Given a chance that I might make a change.
There are some hopes that the
world I can rearrange!
So if you slip and feel that greed.
Just know for you I would bleed!
Not that I'm perfect or anything.
I don't want the world to sing the song I sing.
However I would like to plant a seed.
I just want the world to know that
for you I would Bleed!!!

By
Flame

Flame!

Taking my last breath

People seem to want to bring me down all the time.
I am almost 44 and never seen my prime.
Each individual thinks it's their job
to steal my emotions away.
But even if i am a drunk, i have something to say.
I can see it coming; it's all about my death!
And all I can do is pray for all of you,
as I am taking my last breath.
Desperation, sorrow and pain have walked
back into my life once more.
And there is no answers like before.
Life to other people doesn't seem all that hard.
But that's only because they where
dealt the very best cards.
When you've never slept in a cardboard box.
It is sooo simple to give those positive talks!
And when you never lost all hope.
It's sooo easy to talk about the drunks
and the junkies, who use dope!
And when your freedom has never been taken away.
It's easy to tell people to live that way.
For over 30 years i have prayed for my death.
I pray that i will feel every ounce of pain
as i am taking my last breath.
The guilt i feel of not living up to
what everyone says i should be.
God! Don't you know, it's killing me?
Sleep is nothing more than a nightmare.
And my destiny is nothing more than a dare.
I have trusted my country and loved all the rest.
I have fallen to the ground and watched people
around me hoping I was taking my last breath.
Dear lord, take my life and bring upon me death!
And please! Have mercy on me,
as I am taking my last breath!!!

By
Flame

Flame!

Tear Of a Cloud

I don't understand what's going on, and I don't know why it's allowed.
But this is what I call the tear of a cloud!
My heart has felt many pains.
My feelings are quite frequently refrained.
It is not understood to me why
people get so loud.
But this is what I call a tear of a cloud.
Leave me with emotions I have.
And please don't laugh.
Don't take my pride down.
Just touch the sway of my gown.
And as you bend down.
Taste the tear of a cloud.
And when you hear the skies
scream out loud.
Then you will see the tear of a cloud!!!

By
Flame

Flame!🌹☺

Tears for a Friend

I only knew you for a short while.
And from the beginning I knew you had style.
You liked my poetry and the way I sang.
You helped me solve my problems and every thang.
To me, my problems weren't easy, they were pretty bad.
Yet, you made me feel grateful for everything I had.
When it all came down to the very end.
It seems that I had tears for a friend!
Fortunately, you gave me happiness all the time.
Somehow you always made me feel like I was in my prime.
You were like the Dad; I've missed for many years.
Making me feel good and taking away all my fears.
Life isn't easy, that's what you always let me know.
Always pointing me to the right way to go.
Paul, laying it down on the line to my peers.
For you, I have tears.
Our souls, for a moment, touched.
This doesn't happen too often, not as such.
This could only happen with someone who could care.
And now I'm about to tell you something I just can't bear.
You've been thru life and faced all its fears.
You've had your ups and downs and you've had your tears.
Give me a break, because right to the end,
I've had tears for a friend!
Where ever you are, I know it's the best.
And trust me my friend; I will finish your quest.
You were somebody that always took it to the end.
But, for me, I am left with the tears for a friend.

By
Flame

Flame!🌹☺

The sadness of the wild one

Crazy as he is, he will always totally blow your mind.
Right or wrong, he just wants to be the different kind.
He is not afraid to face a thousand guns.
This is the sadness of the wild one!
Death does not bother him, not at all.
And he cares not about any call.
Never let him think you know him in any way.
Because, he will show you different in every way.
Coolness is not his way that he has already done.
For he is the sadness of the wild one!
If nothing else, he wants to create havoc
in your very little brain.
He doesn't want you to feel crazy, but just
how it feels to be insane.
He's not lonely and his father loved his son.
And yet, he is the sadness of the wild one!!!

By
Flame

Flame!

Belief in You

Life isn't that great.
It's all one great debate.
Hell seems like a fury.
But there is nothing
To the contrary.
Given the day i had.
It really hasn't been that bad.
It isn't easy being somebody I'm not.
Let me ask you how it feels to have what you've got.
There is nothing ever so true.
Then my belief in you.
Give me the life that's enhanced.
Just give me that one last dance.
Romance is something that's flowing out of me.
This is something you have to see.
Please give me a break.
Baby you're giving me heartache.
I don't want to sound 'sad or blue.
There's nothing but belief in you.

By
Flame

Flame! 🙂

Christmas Day

We just can't wait.
I don't know, maybe it's just fate.
I think we just pray.
For that Christmas day!
Things are going to turn out good.
They are going to turn out like they should.
Liston to what I say.
We will have our Christmas day!
Our world is waiting for something
to happen right now.
And the pain will go away, WOW!
No matter what we have to pay.
To see that Christmas day!
Like a child waiting the day before.
We don't really know what for.
But we will awake with absolute dismay.
Because everything will be there on
Christmas day!

By
Flame

Flame!

Crazy Horse

I walked with the Indians many years ago.
They taught me to hunt; they taught me to fish,
they even taught me to sew.
It was such a peaceful thing, there was no remorse.
And get this; the chief's name was Crazy Horse!
With the feathers and the colors in a peaceful way.
I will never forget his knowledge until my dying day.
He must have been crazy, yes indeed.
Because for hatred he always tried to intercede.
And to break it down to you, I will of course.
How can a man like this have
a name like, "Crazy Horse?"
with paint on his face and feathers across his head.
I actually heard the last words he said.
My brother, in order to build up your strength, you must breakdown your force.
At that moment, we did a dance and sang praises to Crazy Horse!!!

By
Flame

Flame!☺

Element

Clocks are running in reverse.
And people no longer know how to converse.
Times are hard and at such a cost.
These days it seems that everything is lost.
The signs from heaven are sent.
What we are looking at is the ELEMENT!
Read your bible and see what I say.
And you will see how things are done today.
Let me try to give you a clue.
It absolutely matters what you do.
Life is something that's inside out.
Just when you think you've got it, you're full of doubt.
And sometimes when we think all
of our time has been spent.
What we really face is the ELEMENT!
How can we look at life in such a simplified way?
When the ELEMENT approaches each day!
Words spoken without meaning at all.
How is it that we are supposed to hear our call.
They say lightning never strikes twice in the same place.
And there are times when you cannot
trust your neighbor's face.
There are things, on this earth, that weren't meant.
Dear God in heaven I know now that we are facing,
the ELEMENT!!!

By
Flame

Flame! ☺

Gods View

I look upon you and I can't understand.
What happened when I created man?
I gave you the moon and stars.
And you took it way too far.
The blue skies I gave you for an aria.
Somehow you turned gray.
This is Gods view open your eyes.
This is Gods view, do not hide.
He loved us before we were made.
And he promised we would always stay.
You kill and mame
You take advantage of the lame.
Who is it that is to blame?
A bullet has been shot out of a gun.
You killed someone and then started to run.
So I might just open the skies.
This is Gods view open your eyes.
This is Gods view, do not hide.
He loved us before we were made.
And he promised we would always stay.
REPEAT.

By
Flame

Flame!

Heaven's shining down

The other morning I looked up at the morning sky.
Thinking I saw you, I started to cry.
The other day I was talking to a neighbor
and thought I saw your face.
I felt awkward and kind of out of place.
Seems like every time I turn around.
Heaven's shining down!
Every time I go to the store I get a lump in my throat.
Because, behind the cashier, I see you start to float.
I was driving pass the store just the other day.
I thought I saw your body moving
in your brisk kind of way.
And once in a while, I hear a funny kind of sound.
It truly makes me feel like heaven's shining down!
I knew when I laid you to rest, I would be missing you.
But I didn't realize just what it would do.
I didn't know that all around town.
The heavens would be shining down!!!

By
Flame

Flame!🌹☺

I Forgot II

I forgot the love you sent in so many ways.
I forgot the sunshine you brought into the days.
I forgot the courage you gave me to go on.
I forgot the bad memories you made gone.
I forgot the green grass under my feet.
I forgot that you told me to forgive deceit.
I forgot the pain that you had taken away.
I forgot the promises you had to say.
I forgot the time you put together for just me.
I forgot the vast and mighty sea.
I forgot how you took away my strife.
I forgot all the people you put in my life.
Sometimes it's hard to remember the things you do.
Like I forgot you gave the whole world to say I love you.
And oh sweetest Lord there's one thing I forgot to say to you.
Simply this . . . . . I Forgot!!!!!!

By
Flame

Flame! ☺

I Need The Trust Back

I've done some things I'm
not proud of.
I mean some real lousy stuff.
And I can only pray.
That you know I'm just not this way.
For days now my brain I've racked.
Honey, I need the trust back.
Don't give me another reason to
Go on like this.
Please let's make up and kiss.
Without you all I can do is lack.
Please! I need the trust back.
Give me time to prove it.
Given the time, I can do it.
I can be the man I used to be.
And goodness once again
You'll find in me.
Let me make you love me
Again no flack.
Honest, I need the trust back.
I love you so much.
Honest honey, I need the trust back!!

By
Flame

Flame!❧☺

Printed in the United States
By Bookmasters